# Wowed! by the Word

## Discovering the Bible's Big Benefits

# Wowed! by the Word

## Discovering the Bible's Big Benefits

Mark Cedar

*Wowed! by the Word: Discovering the Bible's Big Benefits*
© 2019 by Mark Cedar

All rights reserved. No portion of this book may be reproduced, stored in a retrieval system, or transmitted in any form or by any means — electronic, mechanical, photocopy, recording, scanning, or other — except for brief quotations in critical reviews or articles, without the prior written permission of the author at: mc@visitdsc.org.

All Scripture quotations, unless otherwise marked, are taken from the ESV® Bible (The Holy Bible, English Standard Version®), copyright © 2001 by Crossway, a publishing ministry of Good News Publishers. Used by permission.

Book front cover stock photo image #68052472 courtesy of Dreamstime; back cover photo property of the author: book section and chapter graphic image courtesy of clipartpanda.com.

Thunderbird PRESS
P.O. Box 524
Rancho Mirage, CA 92270
thunderbirdpress@dc.rr.com

Library of Congress Control Number: 2019937871

Cedar, Mark
    *Wowed! by the Word: Discovering the Bible's Big Benefits*
    ISBN: 978-7338985-0-8 (paperback)

Printed in the United States of America

*"...Of making many books there is no end..."*

*Ecclesiastes 12:12*

# Contents

| | | |
|---|---|---|
| Introduction | | ix |
| Chapter 1 | Taking God's Word for It | 1 |
| Chapter 2 | But Seriously, Folks | 5 |
| Chapter 3 | Trust is a Must | 11 |
| Chapter 4 | It's Alive! | 15 |
| Chapter 5 | What It's All About | 19 |
| Chapter 6 | Word Up | 25 |
| Chapter 7 | How's Your Love Life? | 29 |
| Chapter 8 | The Bible's Bennies | 33 |
| Chapter 9 | The Smackdown | 39 |
| Chapter 10 | Diving In Daily | 43 |
| Chapter 11 | What God Has to Say (Topic & Verse) | 47 |
| Chapter 12 | Where to Begin? | 55 |
| In Closing | | 59 |
| Appendix / Chapter Discussion Questions | | 61 |

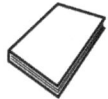

# Introduction

Welcome to a book written entirely about a book. This isn't about just any book, but a text dedicated to arguably the greatest book of all time, the Bible. Maybe you're already familiar with the Bible, or maybe not. Perhaps you've seen it from a distance on a friend's or family member's shelf, found it in a hotel drawer, or walked past a bookstore aisle and there it was—looking at you. Well, this book is about that Book, and it's just for you.

Now, who would write a book about the Bible? You guessed it: a pastor. Not only am I a pastor, but my father as well, and his father, and yes, my great-grandfather, too. Allow me to assure you that my background did not cause me to believe the Bible to be the authentic Word of God. Rather, my heritage simply offered me an exposure to its content. Unlike some who have never cracked open a copy, I was exposed to the Bible regularly. Yet, the decision to accept or reject its unique message and miraculous claims remained a very personal one. In other words, no one forced the Bible down my throat. That no one made me believe it, I can guarantee you. This is worth noting right from the start.

With the writing of *Wowed!* I find myself mildly middle-aged, living a full life in Southern California. My amazing wife, Cheri, and I have two great kids and a crazy dog. And yes, we all love one another. I have a lot to be grateful for, and I dedicate this book happily to them. Additionally, I want to thank our dear friend Jean Denning for expertly editing this text and providing so much valuable counsel for its completion, and Karoline Kessler for converting the manuscript into InDesign and ebook format.

I've been a believer in Jesus Christ for quite a while now, and have experienced many seasons of life—some good, many ordinary and quite a few truly tough. I don't believe it possible to write effectively about the Bible until you have had ample opportunity to test and apply it. While this project has been within my thinking for years, I find myself now realizing that it's time. As a believer in Jesus, I hold the Bible to be the foundational base of all that I engage in—the source for all I have dedicated my life toward. This makes my writing on the topic not only logical, but readily plausible as well. My aim is that these brief pages will stir, engage and challenge you, the reader, toward the highly remarkable content found in the pages of Scripture. I cannot begin to describe how deeply, in times of both deep crisis and ordinary ordeals, I have been impacted and enlightened by what God has to say. If you are a reader who questions the veracity of the Bible's content, I would urge you to stay with me as we take a brief journey together through this wonderful book—*The Book*—that can change your life for the best. Why? Because God wants the best for you, now and forever.

The Bible records history, sharing conquests and defeats. It relates life stories and offers insights for living. It describes creation, the existence of Almighty God and our relationship to Him. It tells us His commands, and offers instruction. Yet, more than anything else, the Bible gives us hope, discovering that God loves us, cares individually for each of us, and gave his own Son to die on our behalf, offering eternal life to all who will believe. Within the Bible's pages, we read of wise king Solomon who related the important words: *"For everything there is a season, and a time for every matter under heaven:"* (Ecclesiastes 3:1). So what time is it right now for you? I don't believe you have this book in your hands by accident or circumstance. Dare I say you have a date with destiny? This is your opportunity to be WOWED! by the Word. I would submit to you that the Bible is not like any other book—not by a long shot. So grab hold of this book with both hands and hang on—here we go!

*"The grass withers, the flower fades,
but the Word of our God will stand forever."*
**Isaiah 40:8**

## Chapter 1: Taking God's Word for It

We begin together with an emphasis on the Word of God. Now it is true that some would call the Bible out of date and old school. Yet it speaks to every situation of life. Some would describe it as violent, hateful and prejudiced. But God says, *"... I have loved you with an everlasting love;"* (Jeremiah 31:3). Romans 2:11 says, *"... For God shows no partiality."* Some would claim the Bible narrow and harsh. Yet in John 10:10, Jesus said, *"I came that they may have life and have it abundantly."* There are those who doubt its divine authority and profound exactitude. But when I read it, it's as if the Bible reads me. Again and again, I discover remarkable wisdom and stirring insight within its pages.

In a recent Gallup study, it was reported that 75% of Americans believe the Bible to be God's Word—that's three-fourths of Americans nationwide. Of that majority number, 28% believe it is the literal Word of God, with the remaining 47% holding it to be an inspired book. Meanwhile, 21% of Americans think the Bible nothing but history and fables. Our culture today would suggest that no one of any mental or social ability would dare think the Bible to be from God. For the reasoning adult, this is a fallacy—a false fabrication designed to dilute the impact of the Word of God today.

The American Bible Society released recent poll results that 77% of Americans say the nation is headed morally downhill, 80% saying they believe the Bible is sacred. The Barna Group has shared that 88% of American households report having at least one Bible in their home. My reason for writing this book is clearly reflected in the related question: How many people actually believe in the Bible today? In other words, is the Bible simply good prose in storybook fashion, or is it the very word of the living God written to us? And if it is God's Word, hadn't we better believe it?

It's nothing new for people to take pot-shots at Scripture. Certainly portions of the Bible can be confusing, while other sections quite uncomfortable. Mark Twain quipped, "It ain't those parts of the Bible that I can't understand that bother me; it is the parts that I do understand." So true. Yet even in the technologically advanced world of the 21st century, the Bible continues to be the best-selling book of all time. Cannot we deduce that if God has determined to communicate with us, He would include some concepts more difficult to grasp? Arguably, we must also accept that God's laws and commands would not always be to our liking. What child always enjoys a parent's instruction? Similarly, what kind of a parent fails to instruct his or her child?

In other words, evaluation of the Bible's authority and origin should not be squarely placed upon the shoulders of "likeability"; i.e., do we enjoy it or want to elect it to public office? If it is God's Word, it is not up to God to align Himself with our opinions, but instead to advise us of His position. Notable author Harper Lee has stated, "The book to read is not the one which thinks for you, but the one which makes you think. No book in the world equals the Bible for that."

If the Bible truly is the Word of God, then it is given for our benefit, providing a powerful dose of supernatural insight from the Almighty for all who will discover and realize its life-changing message. Prepare to be "Wowed! by the Word."

As a side note, keep in mind that the Bible was originally written primarily in Hebrew (Old Testament) and Greek (New Testament). It remains the most largely linguistically translated text worldwide. If you've ever wondered whether God spoke like Shakespeare (Thee, Shalt, Thou), just know that the King James Bible began translation way back in 1604, and was completed and published in 1611. It's still widely revered due to its literal consistency with the original text. For our time together, we'll go with the English Standard Version (ESV®) for its readability, word-for-word literal accuracy, and literary excellence.

*"Every Word of God proves true; ..."*
Proverbs 30:5

### Chapter 2: But Seriously, Folks

If I've heard the statement once, I've heard it a thousand times: "But seriously, folks!" I think it's because of my great love of comedy. Laughing is good for you—it's a medically proven fact! The Bible commends it, stating *"A joyful heart is good medicine ..."* (Proverbs 17:22). (By the way, those words were recorded in Scripture long before medical studies on the benefits of laughter were ever conducted.)

Largely due to the fact that Scripture was completed thousands of years ago, one could intelligently wonder whether it should be taken seriously in our modern world today. After all, the printing press didn't come onto the historical scene until the 15th century, and Amazon only began selling books online in 1995. These realities mixed with intelligent skepticism begs further discussion on the validity of the content of the Bible as we read it today. Can God's Word, as it claims to truly be, actually be trusted?

The Bible is not a text penned by one author, but rather a collection of 66 books written over the course of 1500 years on three separate continents (Africa, Asia and Europe) by 40 different individuals ranging from peasants to kings covering 60 generations. No wonder I'm Wowed! by the Word. Yet, you would be right to question my assertion of there being 40 writers. To the point, my statement is that one author did not pen the Bible, but rather 40 writers did. The interesting thing is that the Bible claims to be inspired by just one author, namely God Almighty. It's interesting that the human writers of each book are often found in the names of the books of the Bible; however, they do not claim to be the inspired author. They simply wrote down what they were inspired by God to record. This is the unique claim of the Bible, as well as the reason why the cover often reads "Holy Bible." It relates to us that it is indeed an inspired book by God. In other words, God desires to communicate with us, and has chosen to do so through His book. Such is the claim of the Bible.

It is not just a book about living, but rather states it is the book of life. The internal consistency of the various books in their content is remarkable. The teaching and account of various writers consistently aligns itself with the whole of the Bible. Even as Jesus Himself recites the writings of Scripture, He relates them to be entirely true and accurate. Modern-day claims of inconsistencies in Scripture are reasonably explainable. For example, the writers of the Gospels included Matthew, Mark, Luke and John. Being a physician, Luke intelligently wrote with intellect, while John as one of the three closest disciples to Jesus often wrote using personal detail. In similar fashion, details of the crucifixion of Christ and His subsequent resurrection on the third day represent key points each writer is uniquely compelled to include. Indeed, if four different authors wrote of the identical details, one would suspect a conspiracy of authorship, much like an alibi story which guilty parties agree together to universally tell. Lastly, just because one author notes a certain fact does not mean another truth is not also equally valid. These realities add credence to the claim of the veracity of Scripture, not weaken it. When reading of the miracles, remember that Jesus multiplied the loaves and fishes more than once—as recorded consecutively in Mark's Gospel. So many times, faulty conclusions are rashly drawn to criticize the Bible without even beginning to intelligently examine its content. Details certainly vary as they should, yet the spiritual teaching of the Bible (its theology) does not conflict within its myriad of pages.

My point is this: the Bible has incredibly strong internal support across its vast and vivid landscape. Historically speaking, there is more evidence, outside of the Bible's pages, that Jesus Christ existed—even more than that of Shakespeare. But back to our topic: the Bible. Interestingly enough, we find again and again in Scripture the claim that its writings are indeed the very word of God:

> *"The law of the Lord is perfect, reviving the soul; the testimony of the Lord is sure, making wise the simple; the precepts of the Lord are right, rejoicing the heart; the commandment of the Lord is pure, enlightening the eyes; the fear of the Lord is clean, enduring forever; the rules of the Lord are true, and righteous altogether. More to be desired are they than gold, even much fine gold; sweeter also than honey and drippings of the honeycomb."*
> —Psalm 19:7–10

> *"And we also thank God constantly for this, that when you received the Word of God, which you heard from us, you accepted it not as the word of men but as what it really is, the Word of God, which is at work in you believers."*
> —1 Thessalonians 2:13

> *"All Scripture is breathed out by God ..."*
> —2 Timothy 3:16

> *"For no prophecy was ever produced by the will of man, but men spoke from God as they were carried along by the Holy Spirit."*
> —2 Peter 1:21

Did you know that 27% of the Bible's content is predictive? In other words, its prophecy forecasts things to come. Interestingly enough, not even Nostradamus comes anywhere close to the perfect track record of the Bible's prophets for predictions coming true. The real tests of prophecy are authenticity and reliability. You can bet on your Bible for that! In fact, the Bible contains over 300 prophecies alone about the coming Messiah, all realized in the person of Jesus Christ. Within Psalm 22 we find graphic detail of how the Messiah would die on a cross, recorded 1000 years before crucifixion was invented by the Romans. Psalm 16 tells us that the Messiah would rise from the dead. For a heavy dose of prophecies fulfilled in Christ, the book of Isaiah is packed with them. It's an amazing thing to consider the claims of the Bible which were made so far ahead of time.

Next we turn to archaeological support for the Bible and its historical accuracy. Interestingly enough, for the past 150 years archaeologists have widely considered the Bible a reliable guide for their digs. By 1958, over 25,000 discoveries were made, each further confirming the historical accuracy of the Bible. In my own travels to Israel, I've stood in the unearthed temple in Capernaum where Jesus often taught, journeyed in King Hezekiah's underground tunnel below Jerusalem, and seen the place of the Skull. In truth, with all of the discoveries supporting Scripture, there has not been one to deny it. Perhaps the greatest discovery of the last century was the 1947 find of the Dead Sea Scrolls in Qumran. There in desert caves, sealed in clay jars, the entire book of Isaiah and portions of every Old Testament book except Esther were found, dating back before the time of Christ. Up to this point, the oldest copies of the Old Testament were dated from 900 AD, but no longer. Meanwhile, more than 5,300 known Greek manuscripts of the New Testament along with 10,000 Latin manuscripts and 9,300 other earlier portions of the New Testament still exist. All of these documents retain incredible consistency. No other documents in antiquity even begin to approach this level of reliability. In fact, Homer's *Iliad* comes next in line for preserved manuscripts at a total count of 634 copies, with the oldest edition from the 13th century. As John Warwick Montgomery has stated, "To be skeptical of the resultant text of the New Testament books is to allow all of classical antiquity to slip into obscurity." Truly, no other writing can compare in record.

In case you wish to debate the historicity of Jesus, try arguing with the 39 sources outside of the Bible which reveal over 100 facts about Christ's life and teachings, his death and his resurrection. Perhaps rejections toward the Bible stem largely from its description of miracles. One must ask: Is there truly no possibility of it? Within science's modern-day theory of evolution, even the most basic estimation of odds for the random formation of life urges the belief in the miraculous. As we read the account of so many miracles performed by Jesus, we find the response of people varying from shock to disbelief, confusion to utter amazement. Would we expect no less? I personally think it takes a lot more faith to believe in the theory of evolution than it takes to believe in a Creator. What a pleasure years ago in Washington, D.C. to hear Dr. Francis Collins of Nobel Prize status remark that more and more scientists, as they peer deeper and deeper into creation to see the remarkable complexities of life, are coming to believe in a Divine Creator. Confronted by the depths of his own genetic discoveries, he embraced God's existence with personal certainty. Here's the rub: the Bible makes emphatically clear that God intends His Word and His existence to be accepted by individuals on the basis of faith—a faith which is reasonable, built upon abundant evidence, strong logic and spiritual sense. It's not a blind leap, but a loving step toward God which He rewards with His presence and assurance. *"but my righteous one shall live by faith, ..."* (Hebrews 10:38). It is faith which is the commodity of heaven.

*"... your Word is truth."*
John 17:17

## Chapter 3: Trust is a Must

The Bible is self-attesting. In other words, it unequivocally declares and continually supports itself as being the very word of God. As the Bible describes God being completely trustworthy and entirely perfect, so His Word is without error or shortcoming as well. In other words, the Bible does not claim to be a heavenly suggestion book, but rather declares itself absolutely, unequivocally true in all its content, a divinely trustworthy sourcebook.

Those who begin to doubt the Bible soon discover that the power, the promise, and the potency of the Word of God have drained right out. The Bible was never intended by God to merely be words on a page, nor a solution for insomnia. It is the most important content you will ever discover for your life. But it must be absorbed in an attitude of absolute trust and reliance. Anything less, and the Bible will be a boring, baffling and begrudging bummer.

I have never forgotten what a friend once told me. He saw me reading my Bible one day, and approached my office desk with this instruction: "Whenever you open the Word of God, ask Him to speak to you, to reveal to you, to make

His Word alive in your life." It changed the way I read my Bible. I began to open the Word of God expectantly, ready to receive what God would relate to me. I soon was asking God to speak directly to me from the pages of His book, and invited Him to help me understand what He was trying to tell me. Suffice it to say, the outcome is that more and more, I have found the words of the Bible to literally leap off the page.

If you doubt the difference God's Word can make in your life, if you struggle believing the Bible's content is written just for you, if you vacillate on the reliability of Scripture and its applicability to your life: get your doubt straightened out!

That's what a man named Billy Graham did. It was 1949, and young Mr. Graham was a graduate of Wheaton College, and planned to speak in a tent meeting in downtown Los Angeles. He arrived in Southern California early, and spent time retreating at a conference center in the San Bernardino mountains. It was there in the moonlight that Billy Graham wrestled with the question of this chapter: Was the Bible indeed the very Word of the living God? He knew he could not speak in Los Angeles, nor continue in any ministry, without facing this question head-on. His memoirs explain that he ultimately placed his Bible on a tree stump and told God that He accepted the Bible as His Word, the very word of the living God. It required a step of faith. And it changed Mr. Graham's life. For in 1949 in Los Angeles, he would gain national reputation, and go on to become the most prominent evangelist and minister of the 20th century.

My friend, as long as you treat the Word of God lightly, you will not amount to much as far as the Kingdom of God is concerned. You may find it handy to compromise on God's laws to advance in business, or to gain temporary desires, but you will not succeed in life. Only when you come under the words of the Bible, God's Basic Instructions Before Leaving Earth, will you begin to find lasting success—and all God desires for you to achieve. Even as Jesus said to Peter, *"O you of little faith, why did you doubt?"* (Matthew 14:31)—so we, too, must settle our quandaries. Until you have become convinced of the Bible's divine authorship, you cannot move into the best chapters of your life. Oh, what the Bible can do for you, if you will simply trust it for all it's worth! Remember, everyone believes something.

The atheist believes that everything around us in nature and within our own beings is simply happenstance, nothing but cosmic chance come true. Now if that's not a big stretch of a belief system, I don't know what is. We are born into this life confronted with the realization of our own existence. Why are we here? What's life all about? How did all this happen? How is it that everything works together? From the Bible's opening page in its first statement in Genesis 1:1, we discover, "In the beginning, God created the heavens and the earth." This declaration reveals a basis for our existence and an identity for our source. The challenge is clear—will we take God seriously? Psalm 53:1 states, *"The fool says in his heart, 'There is no God.'"*

Will you give God's Word a chance? Are you ready to gamble your welfare on the belief that you can never know the answer to life's ultimate questions? The Bible uniquely offers the true answers to our existence which spiritually make sense. I humbly submit to you: it's unquestionably worth taking a good look.

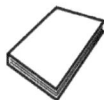

*"For the Word of God is living and active, ..."*
*Hebrews 4:12*

### Chapter 4: It's Alive!

This chapter is suitably titled for the start of an epic Zombie thriller. Thank God we all lived through that craze. Actually, I am amazed by the number of zombies in our world today. There are so many individuals just going through the motions, surviving but not succeeding in life. Some zombies are more enthusiastic and busy, but they are still not taking action on their zombie-like state. They're just more impressive zombies. If we were taking a zombie group photo, we'd probably ask them to stand in the front, near the center of the pack. The Bible teaches that we are all born spiritually dead, and only God can breathe life into us. That's what the Word of God is all about. It's a resuscitation device, given by God, used by the Holy Spirit, to give us life and make us new. And it all works because Jesus died for us on the cross, and rose to make our new life possible. Because He lives, we can too. In the Word of God, we find the truth we need which God will use to foster the new life He offers us. Jesus freely offers our new life, the Holy Spirit supernaturally empowers it, and the Word of God wisely instructs and lovingly guides it all along the way. Remember, it was the band The Zombies who made the hit record in 1965, "She's Not There." The Bible tells us that spiritually speaking, there are many in our world who just aren't really there.

Much earlier in my years, my friends and I would regularly engage in a familiar discussion. On the playground of elementary school, one would always look for something out of the ordinary. From time to time we would find a bug, usually the kind that had a good sting or far too many legs, and soon the discussion would ensue.

"Don't touch it! It's alive!"
"No, it's not."
"Yah, it is. I just saw it move!"
"Poke it and find out."
"I'm not touching it. You do it."

Sometimes the best test of seeing whether something is alive or not is to just plain poke it. So, let's poke at the Bible together. Too many assume the text that claims to be God's Word is a dead, lifeless book, and draw this conclusion before ever examining it. Why not find out, once and for all, whether the Bible is alive. For this is what it claims, written by the very God of the universe, for our understanding. Too many Bibles sit still, on shelves and in drawers, appearing lifeless and of no account. Treated as a document of the past, the book's content goes frequently unattended. Yet, when stirred, it offers insights and teachings beyond comparison. In a modern world of unparalleled discovery and knowledge, the struggles of human nature continue to envelop and deter true advancement. Could it be that we are turning a blind eye to the source we need most? What are we so afraid of? Why not give it a good poke, and see if it moves?

Interestingly enough, the Bible claims to be the very Word of God—given to us. We find within its pages that whenever God speaks, things happen—many of which are impossible by ordinary means. Therefore, we can apply the

*It's Alive!*

spiritual principle that when God speaks and we listen, His living word transfers into our lives, and we are impacted with life. Much like the electrified medical paddles used when someone is in heart failure, we may need a strong jolt to receive the life message He is desiring to impart. Just get ready, for as you poke at His Word, it will poke back at you—in a profound and powerful way.

Perhaps this is why so many steer clear of the Bible—because it profoundly impacts the reader. As a kid, I loved comic books. There was something about the engaging pictures, the entertaining stories, the humor and the action of comics that kept me coming back, time and time again, for more. As I grew, I found that my teachers in school did not share my reading interests. Instead, they assigned readings in books filled with instruction, factual information, and thought. I can honestly say that all the way through graduate school, and into the present day, my life has been impacted by these books, rather than the comics.

Allow me to give you a reading assignment which will truly pay off: read a Bible. Unless it's a children's Bible, it won't have pictures inside, but it will build into your life—much more than you could ever imagine possible. Its stories are true, and its action and humor have lessons attached. It's not superficial, but a book of life-impacting lesson, absolute truth and lasting hope!

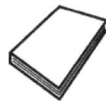

*"'For God so loved the world,
that He gave His only Son,
that whoever believes in Him
should not perish but have eternal life.'"*
*John 3:16*

### Chapter 5: What It's All About

We've waited long enough; it's time to get to the point. Spoiler Alert: I'm about to tell you what the Bible is all about. I mention this because you may want to read the entire 66 books that comprise the Word of God to discover this on your own. But if you're okay with my getting to the point, then please read on.

The Bible is a book of relationship. I know that may sound surprising. Most think of it as a giant list of rules — the "dos" and "don'ts" of life. To be totally clear, it definitely has God's commands for us within its pages. But the overarching message of the Bible is this: God loves us; each and every one of us, and He longs that we enjoy a never-ending relationship with Him. That friendship with God, if you choose to accept it, continues with God forever in heaven. There you have it: the Bible explains how we can enjoy a relationship with God. Now, why would you want to do that? After all, most of us understand that within the description of God we find a supreme being with ultimate power and authority. If we approach God, maybe we will upset Him. Isn't it better to just leave well enough alone? You know: I live my life, and God does His thing.

Allow me to digress: Not too long ago, I came home with a new mobile phone. I needed something new with a decent battery that would run all my apps and handle my connection needs. Here's the rub: it has a super-small screen. Now, I chose this model for an important reason: it had to fit in my front pants pocket. And not only fit in, but come out of that pocket quickly and easily when I need it. Now, when my kids saw my new phone, they naturally asked, "What's with the small screen, Dad? Haven't you seen the latest bevel-edge big-screen model?" But that wouldn't have fit in my front pocket, and I certainly would not have been able to get it out. There were plenty of amazing big-screen options available, but I need my phone in my front pocket or I know there will be a disaster down the road due to my phone-handling technique. Thankfully, the mobile phone store had a smart-phone current model in a small-screen size. It was my one and only good option! Meanwhile, my kids still wonder about me.

Why am I telling you my technology drama? Here's why: We have a big problem, and God has created the solution for it. It's the only working option. It's not what we'd immediately think we need. It's not immediately obvious that we have this problem—we have to read the Word of God to understand it. Signs of our problem are everywhere, but God explains why it's such a problem, and how God determined to solve our problem for us.

If your wheels are turning, you're probably thinking "If He's God, why can't He just easily solve the problem?" The answer is that the problem lies with us. God explains our problem in His Word, the Bible:

> *"for all have sinned and fall short of the glory of God,"*
> —Romans 3:23

To sin is to disobey God. His Word says we've all done it; and frankly, I've been a repeat offender. How about you? From my earliest recollections of childhood, I know I've gone against my parents' instructions, taken things I shouldn't have, not told the truth, and the list goes on and on. (I'm not telling you any more than that!)

Disobeying God is extremely serious. The Bible tells us throughout its content that God is perfect and holy, without fault or error. His environment of heaven is also perfect. Thank God for that. Imagine a heaven that's dysfunctional, or a God who flies off the handle—maybe not every day, but just every 100 years or so. We wouldn't have anything to look forward to, and we surely wouldn't want to live with Him forever! Trust me: a perfect heaven is the only kind of heaven you and I want. The trouble is that we've disobeyed God:

> *"For the wages of sin is death, but the free gift of God is eternal life in Christ Jesus our Lord."*
> —Romans 6:23

The Bible explains that the punishment for living against God is death. This never-ending death is called hell. It is a conscious suffering that goes on and on. But notice that God Himself, in the same sentence explains that we need not experience His punishment. He offers us the gift of His forgiveness, through His Son, Jesus Christ:

> *"but God shows His love for us in that while we were still sinners, Christ died for us."*
> —Romans 5:8

Most every page of the Bible, from the Old Testament all the way through the New, speaks of the need for forgiveness by God, the importance of blood to pay for sin, and the fact that we have disobeyed our Creator. This is why Jesus came, God becoming man, to walk among us—and to die for our sins on the cross:

> *"He Himself bore our sins in His body on the tree, that we might die to sin and live to righteousness. By His wounds you have been healed."*
> —1 Peter 2:24

He was our sacrifice for disobeying God, then He rose again from the dead to show that our sin was paid for, and that we could know God's forgiveness and be at peace with Him:

> *"… if you confess with your mouth that Jesus is Lord, and believe in your heart that God raised Him from the dead, you will be saved."*
> —Romans 10:9

We can be forgiven by God. We do not earn God's forgiveness—it is a free gift God offers each of us:

> *"For by grace you have been saved through faith. And this is not your own doing; it is the gift of God, not a result of works, so that no one may boast."*
> —Ephesians 2:8–9

Like any gift that is offered to us, we must willingly receive it. Have you received Jesus, God's gift of salvation, into your life? If you're willing to admit you have sinned, that you need God's forgiveness, and that you're willing to

*What It's All About*

turn from your sins to live for Him, then talk to God now and settle it. He loves you, and He's listening:

> *Dear Lord Jesus, thank you for loving me. I believe you are God's only Son, that you died for my sins on the cross and rose from the dead so I can live with you forever in heaven. Please forgive me of everything, and come into my life. I'm willing to give up my old ways to live for you. Amen.*

Once you've said "Yes" to God by accepting His Son, Jesus, into your life, you're ready to really enjoy the Bible's content in its entirety! Remember, you're not forgiven by how well you live for God; rather, you are forgiven because of Jesus dying for you, so now you want to live for Him! Know that God always keeps His word, and He has this to say:

> *"But to all who did receive Him, who believed in His name, He gave the right to become children of God,"*
> —John 1:12

> *"Whoever has the Son has life; whoever does not have the Son of God does not have life. I write these things to you who believe in the name of the Son of God that you may know that you have eternal life."*
> —1 John 5:12-13

So there you have it. The truth about real life. We gain it by being forgiven by God through His Son. Jesus is the one who alone can save us. All we need to do is come to Him:

> *"Jesus said to him, 'I am the way, and the truth, and the life. No one comes to the Father except through Me.'"*
> —John 14:6

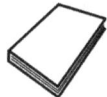

*"'... Man shall not live by bread alone, but by every word that comes from the mouth of God.'"*

Matthew 4:4

## Chapter 6: Word Up

There's nothing like a fish taco ... or a teriyaki burger, or good meatloaf. Don't forget spaghetti and meatballs, wonton soup, and fresh sushi. I've probably made you hungry by now, so forgive me—and just go get a snack. I'll wait. Because we're about to talk about eating the Word of God. That's a figurative statement by the way—don't stick a Bible in your mouth. But when it comes to the Bible ... just eat it!

We have discussed the value of the Word of God, the reliability and truthfulness of its content, and the wonder-working effect it can have upon a life. Now, we shall become strategic in its application to an intensity not yet described.

When one becomes sick, good rest and eating right become priorities. In addition, one may need accurate diagnosis of a condition and the right treatment of the affliction which may include added daily vitamins or medication in regular dosage. The objective is health and vitality, and this worthy goal can be advanced and aided by these strategic, disciplined measures.

The Word of God has the ability to bring great assistance to our lives if we will simply employ it. Sitting on our shelf, the Bible is a wonderful leather-covered paper weight. However, by using the content given to us by God, we can discover and apply much benefit. For example, what do you draw upon when considering an important decision? Perhaps you would reflect upon your own insight, ask the counsel of a friend or companion, weigh logic, make a list of pros and cons, or follow your heart or intuition. Here's another question to consider: When difficulty arises, how does it affect your countenance? You may hope for the best, try to keep a stiff upper lip, maintain a positive attitude, or resign yourself to fate. I think you get the idea, so let's move on.

Now, consider what God's Word offers you: wise advisement, level-thinking, power-packed encouragement and 24/7 support. All believers should be availing themselves of all the Bible affords them. Sadly, too many believers today are simply settling for leftovers in life. Imagine a vast buffet, stretching out upon a table as far as you can see. You step up with your large empty plate and help yourself to some dry croutons. As you remember what a vast buffet you are meant to enjoy, you scoop another helping of croutons onto your plate. Yours is a rather dry and unsatisfying experience considering all that is available to you. At some point in your tasteless, monotonous meal you may just plain quit eating altogether. Such is the idea of simply hearing standard comments about the Bible from others, but never digging into its rich and diverse content for oneself. Where would the culinary arts be if there was nothing but croutons available to us? Have you heard just enough Bible content to imagine it lifeless and dull (much like a stale crouton), or are you tasting enough of the Bible to enjoy its rich variety and full flavor?

The entire point of being exposed to the Bible is getting its diverse and engaging content down into you, where it can be readily tasted, enjoyed, swallowed and digested. The more you eat, the better you will feel, and the more you will grow and develop a greater desire for it. Conversely, the more you set your Bible aside, and turn to your TV, the Internet, and movies for support and enjoyment, the more you will crave them instead. Eat what's best for you — the very word of the living God. It's packed full of life-giving nutrients, and the only indigestion you'll receive will be good for you in the long run.

*"'... and Your words became to me
a joy and the delight of my heart, ...'"*
*Jeremiah 15:16*

## Chapter 7: How's Your Love Life?

Travel back in time to March 24, 1956 in Chicago, when a song like no other in driving rhythm declared, "Who do you love?" Numerous renditions followed over the decades by groups like Ronnie Hawkins and the Hawks (1963), Quicksilver Messenger Service (1969), the Doors (1970) and George Thorogood and the Destroyers (1978). In its originally recorded release, Bo Diddley sang "Who do you love?" twenty-two times in far less than three minutes. Now that's something to think about.

You can guess what I'm about to urge you to do: Get a love for the Word of God. I don't know what "Wows" you. Growing up in my generation, it was supposed to be sex, drugs and rock 'n roll. As you can tell by the title of this book, I want the Bible to start wowing you. It has the ability to do it, big time!

Interestingly enough, we tend to actively foster a love for whatever interests us. If you like cars, you start reading car magazines, watching car shows, attending car events, tinkering, repairing, restoring and collecting. Soon, you're head over heels with automobiles! I loved my first car, a baby blue Triumph Spitfire convertible. You've got to love any car with a soft top and a bonnet hood. My point is that we can apply this same "love" equation to any area of interest. As you read the Word of God, and as you get into a habit of going back to the Word of God, and as you start to reflect on the Word of God and apply the Word of God and memorize it, you grow in your desire for it. Soon, it will be popping off the page at you—calling for your undivided attention! You, too, can fall in love with God's Word—and it will be a love affair that is well worth your time and attention!

Keep in mind that there is a force working against your love for the Bible. For its pages describe not only the Lord, but the devil as well—whose desire is that you crash and burn in life. Unlike another love in life, your desire for God's Word will continually be challenged and discouraged by the devil, that fallen angel from heaven who thought himself better than the rest and greater than God Himself. He will offer you other reading material and averted interests to take your mind off the topic of God's Word. Don't let him dissuade you. There is a world of blessing awaiting you, as you learn and apply the Word of the living God who loves you and wants what is best for you all along life's journey.

The Bible teaches that we are created to love—both to give it and receive it. The question is where our love interest will land. In other words, where will we place our affections and seek to draw love in return? This is the basis of a healthy marriage, a solid friendship, a rewarding career. But nothing can equal the benefits of placing our affections squarely upon the message of love God has given to us—His holy Word. Cultivate a true love for the one book that loves you back—the Bible.

While it's true that love can hurt, it is incredibly worth it. I'd be a liar not to admit that some of God's words to us are hard to handle. It's not because they're harsh or uncaring, but just the contrary: because God loves us, He tells us some tough things to hear. For example, the first chapter of the book of Romans urges us away from godless living, which may hit close to home. 1 Corinthians, chapter 6, very directly instructs us to steer clear of sexual immorality; and by contrast, chapter 13 defines real love and its selflessness— which is pretty challenging. Then there's Matthew's Gospel, where Jesus shares His "Sermon on the Mount." There on the hillside by the Sea of Galilee, Jesus relates, *"But I say to you, Love your enemies and pray for those who persecute you, ..."* (Matthew 5:44). As quickly as we can deal with the conundrum of loving those who are vehemently against us, Jesus continues by saying, *"Do not lay up for yourselves treasures on earth, where moth and rust destroy, and where thieves break in and steal, but lay up for yourselves treasures in heaven, where neither moth nor rust destroys and where thieves do not break in and steal. For where your treasure is, there your heart will be also."* (Matthew 6:19-21). As we shake our heads in amazement, and seek to wrap our minds around this teaching, we find chapter 7 begin with his declaration, *"'Judge not, that you be not judged. For with the judgment you pronounce you will be judged, and with the measure you use it will be measured to you.'"* Ouch! I guess I needed all that.

I have found that many of the times I struggle with taking opportunity to read the Bible, it is because I don't really want to hear anything challenging or difficult. The truth be told, we need to hear the truth told to us. Proverbs 27:6 states, *"Faithful are the wounds of a friend; ..."* Rest assured, anytime God has something in His Word to say that's tough, it's because He loves us too much to keep it from us. What I'm saying is this: the Bible's content, taken into our lives, will ALWAYS be worth it—unlike the countless episodes of *Gilligan's Island* I watched on TV as a kid. Every single week, they just ended up back on that same old lonely island. God wants to get us off the island of self, sailing forward in the adventure of our lives with Him! But when you're lost, you need a map. That's the Bible—the direction of God for our lives.

*"'... I have treasured the words of His mouth more than my portion of food.'"*
Job 23:12

## Chapter 8: The Bible's Bennies

When we choose to apply the Word of God within our lives, a world of good begins to happen. Suffice it to say, we must hear the Word so that we can apply it. I'm talking here about truly "hearing" it. In other words, we must read the Word, listen to accurate teaching from the Word, personally study the Word, and dwell upon the content of the Word. And for the interested individual, the true student of the Bible, insights come and clarity emerges. The Bible is unlike any other book.

I am not going to rant, nor do I constantly post online what I'm about to relate. What I share here is tremendously relevant and vital to our conversation about the Word of God and its impact upon our lives. Are you ready for it?

The Bible is minimized in our world. Those who quote it are typically viewed as fanatical, out of touch or extreme. Sure, there are nuts out there. I think I may be related to some of them. Back to point: There are reasons for this squelching of the Word of God. The overarching reality is spiritual in nature. God's Word is supernaturally powerful; it is completely true and offers radical life change. This brings us to several inalterable realities about the Bible:

First, there are spiritual forces at work, seeking to keep you from its content. The Bible teaches that this life is our opportunity to decide, either for or against God and His ways. While God's Holy Spirit is urging you toward knowing the Lord of all, the devil is conversely trying to push you away. He will stop at nothing to divert, derail or detain you from reading God's book, because he knows its spiritual power and the pure truth it contains. Jesus spoke of the devil in John 8, verse 44: *"'... He was a murderer from the beginning, and does not stand in the truth, because there is no truth in him. When he lies, he speaks out of his own character, for he is a liar and the father of lies.'"*

Many are buying the lies about God, His Son and His Word, to their own calamity. Don't take a prejudicial view of Scripture—read it for yourself, and get ready to be blessed!

Second, the Bible will challenge you to the core of your being for the ultimate direction of your life. Simply put, it is a life-changing book. I'm not talking about a "tear-jerker" that makes you feel special for a few days, nor am I suggesting it will give you a little inspiration to want to give to the needy every so often, or decide to let a bad habit go. It's way beyond all that. When you read it, you're risking really living large, for it will call out to the depths of your being, and urge you to step into a manner of living that risks one's life and welfare—all because of God's great love and the incredible promise of eternal life that makes everything more than worth it.

Third, you will ultimately receive the Bible entirely or reject it fully—perhaps immediately, or more likely a little bit at a time, over the course of your years. Why? Because it's not natural to love, or give, or sacrifice. It's scary to risk everything for God, to literally give one's life away to his or her Creator. Jesus said repeatedly, again and again throughout

His ministry, *"Follow Me."* Are you ready for that? I had to make my decision, and so will you. Personally, I came to realize that everyone follows someone or something. I'll take Jesus, and everything He offers. Therefore, my advice when you read the Word of God is this: Swallow it. Every single bit of it.

Fourth, I should mention here that ignorance is not bliss when it comes to the Bible. We sometimes avoid the Bible's content because we seem to inherently know that there will be challenging words within its pages. We may believe that not knowing solves this dilemma; but to the contrary, it creates unnecessary damages in life. It's much like hating highway traffic. If you live where I grew up in Orange County, Southern California, it means you don't like the 405 or 91 freeways at rush hour—not on any day of the week. But you can't close your eyes and plow ahead at 5 pm on a workday (at least, you shouldn't take this approach). Rather, the more information you can get about road conditions, and the better you can use every skill you've learned in driving well, the better your trip home, and the less chance of injury or even (dare I say it) fatality. God doesn't give His words to us to wreck our day or depress us in life. He gives us counsel in His word so that we can get home well. I'd rather know what I'm getting into than just facing the wreaked havoc later. Like the great philosopher Forrest Gump has said, "Stupid is as stupid does." This life principle actually came from the Bible in Proverbs 14:12: *"There is a way that seems right to a man, but its end is the way to death."* We all need God's advice—desperately.

Finally, keep in mind that the Bible must be quoted, noted and applied. It's not enough to just rail through its pages as quickly as possible, like swallowing bad-tasting cough medicine. We can accept that its content is good for us while still wanting to hurry up and be done with it. This strategy reminds me of my elementary school days, with the study habit of flying through my assigned readings, then mustering all the intelligence I could for quizzes and tests, finally telling myself that I'd do better next time. My point is to take your time, be still, and really take the Bible in. Make notes, even in the margins, and underline all you want. Soon you'll have favorite verses and words of insight that you've discovered—all ready to apply to your life.

When it comes to getting the Bible's benefits into your life, nothing beats the vital strategy of application. It is when we apply the Bible personally that we see the benefits begin to come in! It is within this strategy of application that one finally realizes the value of committing key verses from the Bible to memory. Yup, I just said it: Scripture memorization. I know you didn't see that coming, but what a great thing to do! Whenever you get a "golden nugget" of Scripture (a statement from God that especially applies to you) then you sure don't want to lose it. In fact, just like a precious jewel, you want to be able to draw it back out and enjoy it time and time again. That's where memorizing a verse comes in.

A great place to begin is with John 3:16 (the title verse at the beginning of chapter 5). Everyone can benefit greatly by memorizing that God loves us so much that He gave His only Son Jesus to die for us so that we can receive the gift of God's forgiveness and heaven. The other benefit of memorizing a verse is that not only can you enjoy it whenever you need, but you can share it with others whenever they need it!

After learning John 3:16, why not next choose verses to memorize based upon what "WOWS" you. Go with the verses that leap off the page, that speak to your spirit, that bring life to your soul. You may ask, "How do I memorize a verse in the Bible?" Here's what I suggest:

| | |
|---|---|
| Step #1 | Find your verse to commit to memory. Get a really good one. |
| Step #2 | Print the verse clearly on a card, post-it note, or slip of paper. |
| Next Step | Give up! (Just kidding—don't stop now! You can do it!) |
| Step #3 | Use the simple system of repetition. You're done. |

What I mean by step #3 is that you will either stop before trying to memorize a verse, or you will get smart and use the simple plan that our brains are wired for—repetition. At the risk of repeating myself, let me say it again: use repetition. This means making the simple commitment to read the verse each day. Within about 30 days, you will know the verse (assuming you're not trying to memorize all of Psalm 119 in one step). My advice is to take it a single verse at a time. Years ago, I began carrying a little clear keychain frame on my key ring. I slide my current verse to memorize into the clear frame (which is attached to my key ring) and then just read it every time I use my keys. That means every time I lock or unlock my house door, I read my verse once. Every time I enter or exit my car, I read my verse once. You get the idea. Believe me, it works. In a similar fashion, stick your verse on a post-it note and place it on your bathroom mirror. When you brush your teeth, morning and night please, just read your verse once. Place a verse card below your TV screen or beside your computer monitor at work. Each time you sit down, read the verse once. It really is that simple, and soon you will have a lot of God's benefits packed into you! You may have another memorization system, so just use what works best. The important thing is to get the Bible from your hands, through your eyes, into your head and down to your heart. Memorization helps you keep it there.

There you have it, and we close yet another chapter together! It's taking advantage of the Bible's benefits that will keep you coming back for more!

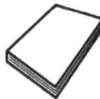

*"All Scripture is breathed out by God and profitable for teaching, for reproof, for correction, and for training in righteousness,"*
2 Timothy 3:16

## Chapter 9: The Smackdown

Growing up, I can remember watching great boxing matches on television. There was no one like Mohammed Ali, who flew like a butterfly and stung like a bee. When he landed a punch, every single person watching personally felt it. I sure know I did. Pow!

There are times, when reading the Bible, that you will feel it speaking directly to you. Whether it's easy to take or hard to swallow, the fact remains: this is a very good thing because it means that God is zeroing in upon an important matter. Many times I have asked, "God, please speak to me." Often to my surprise, He does. It's a quiet yet profound awareness that sweeps over me, too wise and settling and direct to be my own thought. I never cease to be thrilled by statements in His Word that directly address my situations, my concerns, my quandaries, my actions. I would describe any occasion where God gets my attention as a "smackdown" moment. It's like I'm being hit square-on by a loving fist of power and challenge, at just the right intensity. Knocked down, but not knocked out. The traditional term for this God-given experience is called "conviction." It's an intense dose of reality from the holy throne room of God. We will be tempted to deny, dismiss or derail it. Yet our proper response to God's Word is vitally important. We are told to bow down in our spirit, readily admit our need and yield to it. Get ready for a good, loving smackdown from God!

Always remember that nothing derails our personal experience with the Bible more than pride. This topic is addressed readily within Scripture, noting our need to humble ourselves and be open to what God would say to us. In other words, if you're not interested in listening to God, His Word will seem distant. It's as simple as that. What's the use of reading God's life-changing book if you're not open to change?

Perhaps the content of the Bible is lifeless to you. It may seem like stone. Let me advise that reading a current translation of the Bible may relieve some of this dilemma. However, of more likelihood than all else, you may need to prepare your heart and mind to receive what God would say. I'm suggesting here that humility goes a long way for effectively receiving what God offers to impart. We read in the New Testament book of 1 Peter 5:5: "'... *God opposes the proud but gives grace to the humble.*'" A big part of learning from the Lord is being ready and willing. What coach wants us to say we don't need their input, or that we've already become an expert? Even worse, we'd never tell them we don't really want to improve. 1 Peter 5:6 continues: "*Humble yourselves, therefore, under the mighty hand of God so that at the proper time He may exalt you.*" With God, the way up in life is by getting down — just far enough to pay attention and admit you don't have all the answers. Think of it this way:

The further you get down, the easier it is to look up. Proverbs 11:2 states, "... *with the humble is wisdom.*" There is no better life coach than God. He knows our end from our beginning, our interests and our needs. He made us and knows us full well. (See Psalm 139 for a full description of His intimate involvement in each of our lives.)

As a dad, I can tell you that I've always wanted good for my kids. At times, that has involved some hard conversations — much like my dad needed to have with me. It's not because I want to hurt my kids, but instead it's because I love them and have their best interests at heart. Let me tell you: God, your heavenly Father, wants good for you. And He offers you all He has to offer! Just understand that sometimes our God has to bring a hard conversation to the table, for our best! It's because He loves us so much that I can urge you to listen up! *"a bruised reed He will not break, ..."* (Isaiah 42:3). It will always be for your ultimate benefit.

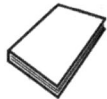

*"Like newborn infants,
long for the pure spiritual milk,
that by it you may grow up
into salvation—"*

1 Peter 2:2

## Chapter 10: Diving In Daily

Our ultimate, most valuable commodity is Time. In this chapter, I will endeavor to convince you to use a portion of it, each day, toward getting into the Bible. So why dive into the Word of God each day? Because it's so worth it! It refreshes us, relieves us, exercises us (stretching our understanding), and urges us on to another rousing lap in the pool of life. It was President Abraham Lincoln who said, "I am busily engaged in the study of the BIBLE. I believe it is God's Word because it finds me where I am."

The big question in our country today is: what are we doing with our Bibles? What do we really believe? And why, in a land where the Bible is so available, are we sliding downhill so fast? Consider with me for a moment the impact the Bible can make upon a life. Jesus spoke about this in the book of Matthew:

> *"'Everyone then who hears these words of Mine and does them will be like a wise man who built his house on the rock. And the rain fell, and the floods came, and the winds blew and beat on that house, but it did not fall, because it had been founded on the rock.'"*
> — Matthew 7:24-25

Next, verses 26-27 explain the foolishness of the life not built on God's Word, and that it will ultimately collapse and fail. You can take this warning to heart, or you can laugh it off.

I've lived long enough to discover that people sometimes joke about the Bible. They make light of it. But don't worry, because God has a sense of humor! I know it, because He made me. (Maybe you can relate.)

So, which man in the Bible had no parents?
*Joshua, son of Nun.*

What kind of man was Boaz before He married Ruth?
*Ruthless.*

Who was the greatest comedian in the Bible?
*Samson. He brought the house down.*

Who was the greatest financier in the Bible?
*Noah. He was floating his stock while everyone else was in liquidation.*

So we can laugh. But don't laugh at God's commands, His claims, His insights and instructions. We need to take His word seriously, because it's stable ... it's sure ... it's strong ... and it's the only thing worth building your life on.

*Diving In Daily*

As you read the Bible, you quickly discover it is a book of relationship between God and mankind. And within it He says I love you, I care about you, and I want you to be at peace with Me. Then it describes how we can know God through His Son Jesus Christ. So allow me to ask the critical question: What will you build your life upon? In other words, on what will you anchor, secure, base, and center yourself?

While we all need to apply good common sense to living, should that be all we've got? Proverbs 28:26 states, *"Whoever trusts in his own mind is a fool, ..."* We can go with society and culture's popular solutions, yet Proverbs 16:25 warns: *"There is a way that seems right to a man, but its end is the way to death."* It was Jesus who said, in Matthew 7, to take the Word of God as your foundational source for living. It will strengthen you, establish you, and keep you—through whatever you face in life.

Arguably, good advice is worth dwelling on. We should think it through, if only for our own best interest. Imagine an entire book that has nothing but the best of advice. That is the Bible. This is why every day should include a reading of God's Word. Personally, I begin the day with a time of prayer and Bible reading. I'm not a "morning person," so I read from The Living Bible (TLB) early each day. It's conversational in nature, and easy to follow. For my study in God's Word, I refer most often to the New American Standard Bible Version (NASB) for its literal translation. My point is this: read it! Not all of it in a single day—good luck with that one! Just set aside a specified time each day to take in a fresh amount! You can start your day with Bible reading, or time at lunch, before dinner, or as you tuck into bed. The important thing is to just do it! Schedule a time in God's Word and stick with the plan. Better to have five minutes a day in the Bible than none at all. Ten minutes a day is even better. You get the point. Get going with your Bible reading, a bit at a time, and soon you'll be adding more and more!

As we conclude this chapter, please remember the key principle of applying advice: Always consider the source. It was Napoleon who stated, "The Bible is not merely a book; it is a living being ..." It's in that mindset that I close with these sourced statements about the Word of God:

> "... *the Word of the Lord proves true;* ..."
> —Psalm 18:30

> "*I have stored up Your Word in my heart, that I might not sin against You.*"
> —Psalm 119:11

> "'... *If you abide in My Word, you are truly My disciples, and you will know the truth, and the truth will set you free.*'"
> —John 8:31-32

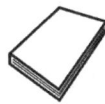

> *"so shall My Word be
> that goes out from My mouth;
> it shall not return to Me empty,
> but it shall accomplish that which
> I purpose, and shall succeed
> in the thing for which I sent it."*
> Isaiah 55:11

### Chapter 11: What God Has to Say

God has much to say to you, as found in the 66 books that comprise the content of His Word. Just remember: God also has much to say to you personally, for whatever you are facing in life. He loves you, and longs to encourage you, guide you, and give you hope and truth for where you are and all you face.

Many people have never realized the potential of God's Word to encourage them, empower them, direct and instruct them, heal them and give them strength. It all starts with mining out those verses that speak to whatever you are facing. Then, taking the verses in and allowing them to work in your life. Every Word of God requires faith — trust that He means business, and that He can do what He says. If you will take His Word in, receive it seriously, and willingly apply it personally, the outcome will be amazing.

Whenever you are seeking answers from the Bible, ask God to direct you to His special word for you — that verse or passage (string of verses) that is applicable.

Provided in this chapter is a brief list of verses from His Word on a wide variety of topics. The Bible verse references given are gems — jewels of truth and understanding that can make a world of difference. So grab a Bible, or turn on your Bible App, and start digging into God's Word for you. That's right — for you!

Note: Each verse listed is categorized only under one theme, although it may apply to many areas. Similarly, this sampling of Scripture references by category is not comprehensive, but includes many of this author's favorites.

### Accountability
*Psalm 69:5; Psalm 139:1–12; Hebrews 4:13; Hebrews 9:27*

### Anger
*Isaiah 54:17; Romans 12:19–21; Ephesians 4:26–27; James 1:19–20*

### Blessing
*Psalm 33:22; Psalm 35:27; Proverbs 3:13; 1 Peter 3:9*

### Comfort
*Psalm 23:1–3; Psalm 30:5; Matthew 5:4; Matthew 11:28*

### Contentment
*Psalm 31:1; Proverbs 14:30; Proverbs 17:22; 1 Timothy 6:6; Hebrews 13:5*

## Courage
*Joshua 1:9; Psalm 27:14; Psalm 31:24; John 16:33*

## Death
*Psalm 23:4; Psalm 116:15; Ecclesiastes 3:1–2; John 11:25; Romans 14:8*

## Difficulty
*2 Corinthians 12:9–10; 1 Peter 5:7; 2 Timothy 3:12*

## Discouragement
*Joshua 1:9; Psalm 42:5; Lamentations 3:19–26*

## Encouragement
*Psalm 54:4; Philippians 1:6; 2 Thessalonians 3:3*

## Endurance
*1 Corinthians 15:58; Galatians 6:9; 1 Timothy 6:12; Hebrews 12:1–4; 1 James 5:11*

## Faith
*Jeremiah 32:26; Acts 16:31; 2 Timothy 1:12; Hebrews 10:38; Hebrews 11:1,6*

## Fear
*Psalm 27:1; Proverbs 28:1; Proverbs 29:25; Romans 8:31; 2 Timothy 1:7*

## Forgiveness
*Matthew 18:21–35; Ephesians 4:32; 1 Peter 4:8; 1 John 1:8–10*

## Fun
*Ecclesiastes 11:9; John 10:10; 1 Corinthians 10:31; Philippians 4:4*

## Giving
*Proverbs 11:25; Malachi 3:10; Luke 6:38; 2 Corinthians 9:6–8*

## God
*Deuteronomy 6:4–5; Psalm 19:1; Isaiah 6:3; Romans 1:20*

## Gospel
*John 3:16–17; Romans 1:16; Romans 10:9; 2 Corinthians 15:3–4*

## Grace & Mercy
*Romans 8:1–2; Ephesians 2:8–9; Hebrews 4:16*

## Guidance
*Psalm 32:8; Psalm 37:23; Proverbs 3:5,6; Jeremiah 29:11; Matthew 6:33*

## Guilt
*Psalm 103:8–12; Acts 13:39; Romans 8:1–2; 1 John 1:9*

## Heaven
*John 3:36; John 5:24; John 14:1–6; Romans 5:1; Romans 10:13; 1 John 5:11–13*

## Holy Spirit
*Micah 3:8; Galatians 5:16–25; Ephesians 3:16; Ephesians 5:18*

## Hope
*Psalm 39:7; Psalm 42:5; Lamentations 3:24; Romans 15:13; Colossians 1:27; Hebrews 6:19; Hebrews 10:23*

## Humility
*Psalm 138:6; Daniel 4:37; Galatians 6:14; James 4:6,10; 1 Peter 5:5-6*

## Immorality
*Psalm 101:3; 1 Corinthians 6:13-20; 1 Thessalonians 4:3*

## Intoxication
*Proverbs 23:29-35; Isaiah 5:22; Ephesians 5:18*

## Jesus
*John 1:1,14; John 14:6; Acts 2:36; Acts 4:12; 2 Corinthians 5:19; Colossians 1:15-20; Colossians 2:9; 1 Timothy 2:5-6*

## Life
*John 10:10; John 14:6; Romans 12:2; Romans 14:8; 2 Corinthians 5:17*

## Love
*Jeremiah 31:3; John 3:16; 1 Corinthians 13:1-8; 1 Corinthians 16:14; 1 John 3:1; 1 John 4:7-8, 19*

## Marriage
*Genesis 2:24; Proverbs 5:15-23; Galatians 5:13; Ephesians 4:26-32; Ephesians 5:22-33; Colossians 3:18-21; 1 Peter 3:1-9; 1 Peter 4:8*

## Miracle
*Jeremiah 32:26; Jeremiah 33:3; Matthew 7:7; Luke 1:37*

## Money
*Psalm 62:10; Matthew 6:24–34; Matthew 10:17–27;
Ecclesiastes 5:10; Hebrews 13:5; 1 Timothy 6:6*

## Need
*Psalm 55:22; Psalm 107:9; Ephesians 3:20; Philippians 4:19*

## Obedience
*Mark 8:34; Romans 6:11; Philippians 1:27; Colossians 2:6*

## Parenting
*Proverbs 22:6; Proverbs 29:17; Ephesians 6:1–4;
Hebrews 12:11*

## Perseverance
*Proverbs 24:10; 2 Corinthians 4:16–18; Philippians 3:13–14;
James 1:2–4; Revelation 12:11*

## Possessions
*Psalm 37:4; Psalm 62:10; Psalm 84:11; Mark 8:36–37;
Luke 12:15*

## Prayer
*Psalm 145:18; Romans 8:26–27; Ephesians 6:18;
1 Thessalonians 5:17; James 5:16*

## Prejudice
*Acts 10:34-35; Romans 2:11; 1 Timothy 2:4*

## Pride
*Psalm 138:6; Proverbs 16:18-19; James 4:6-10; 1 Peter 5:5-6*

## Salvation
*Isaiah 55:6-7; John 1:12; John 3:16-17; Acts 16:31; Romans 5:8; Romans 10:9; Ephesians 2:8-9; Hebrews 7:25; Revelation 3:20*

## Sin
*Isaiah 53:6; Romans 3:23; Romans 6:23; Romans 12:9; 1 Corinthians 15:34; Hebrews 9:27*

## Strength
*Psalm 31:24; Isaiah 40:31; Ephesians 6:10-18; Philippians 4:13*

## Service
*Psalm 100:2; Isaiah 43:10; Galatians 2:20; Colossians 3:23-24*

## Temptation
*Proverbs 23:17-18; 1 Corinthians 10:13; Galatians 6:7-9; James 4:7-8*

## Thankfulness
*Ephesians 5:20; Philippians 4:4; 1 Thessalonians 5:18*

## Victory
1 John 4:4; 1 John 5:5; Romans 8:37; Romans 16:20;
1 Corinthians 15:57; 2 Corinthians 2:14

## Wisdom
Proverbs 1:7; Proverbs 2:1–15; 1 Corinthians 1:25; James 1:5

## Witness
Mark 1:17; Mark 16:15; Acts 1:8; Romans 1:16;
Colossians 4:5–6; 2 Corinthians 5:20; 1 Peter 3:15

## Worry
Psalm 42:5; Psalm 46:10; Romans 8:28; Philippians 4:6–7;
1 Peter 5:7

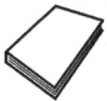

*"How sweet are Your words to my taste, sweeter than honey to my mouth!"*
*Psalm 119:103*

### Chapter 12: Where to Begin?

Whoever invented the buffet dinner was a genius! Yum! An entire smorgasbord of delightful dishes set side-by-side and so hot, ready and waiting. All you have to do is step up, make your selections to fill your plate, and dine to your delight! I've been to a few buffets where I've been so overwhelmed by the quality and selection that I found myself thinking, "Where do I begin?"

The Bible's 66 books, found hot and ready, served up side-by-side, offer a similar dilemma. The obvious question we must ask ourselves is "Where do I begin?" The previous chapter provided a variety of topics with individual verse references which is useful for receiving the Bible's help on a wide array of topics which personally impact us all. When it comes to planning our general Bible reading, it's another matter because of the enormous amount of content before us. The English Bible contains roughly 700,000 words. That's a lot to digest! As we stand before the delicious buffet of God's Word, allow me to make a few dining recommendations of where to start.

If a dinner salad or cup of soup is your pleasure, the book of Genesis is a great place to start. As the first book found in the Bible, it records the creation of the world, the beginning of mankind, and incredible stories about individuals like Adam and Eve, Noah, Abraham, Sarah, Isaac, Rebekah, Jacob, King Pharaoh and Joseph. Immediately after Genesis is the book of Exodus, containing the story of Moses, the Ten Commandments and the Children of Israel. (No one can argue that Charlton Heston did an amazing job of acting out the book of Exodus in the classic film directed by Cecil B. DeMille, *The Ten Commandments*.)

For low-calorie intake that's really good for you, read the Psalms which are located almost exactly in the middle of your Bible. They relate praises to God, prayers for the Lord's protection, and comforting words of hope and encouragement. Personally, I try to include some Psalms in my own Bible reading every day, primarily because they pick me up and keep me going!

If you want some protein in your diet, go over to Proverbs (immediately after the Psalms) where you'll find wise saying after wise saying, predominantly written by King Solomon under the inspiration of God. God's Word tells us he was the wisest king who ever lived, as well as the wealthiest. You will quickly become captivated by evaluating your own stance and approach to life in relation to the wise advice found in this profound book. Many best-selling business books today relate the timeless principles found here in the book of Proverbs, recorded thousands of years ago.

For the real meat and potatoes of the Bible, go to the first four books of the New Testament: Matthew, Mark, Luke and John. These four books relate the life and ministry of Jesus Christ including his birth, upbringing, miracles, teaching, death, rising from the dead, and ascending into heaven. The Bible points consistently to the coming Messiah (Savior of the world), which is found in Jesus. Anyone considering the claims of Jesus, or the validity of the Bible, or God's importance in his or her life should begin reading here. Jesus gets right to the point!

The side dishes of our meal include the letters to the early church (most of the remaining books of the New Testament) and the history of God's people throughout the Old Testament.

Finally, for an amazing dessert, go through the Bible's final book of Revelation. It speaks prophetically of the coming again of Jesus Christ, which many of us believe will be very, very soon! Just keep in mind that it's a very apocalyptic book, so one need not fear the future if you've accepted Jesus into your life. For more on knowing Jesus personally, review chapter five. While the book of Revelation describes the Apostle John's heavenly vision in very figurate terms, keep in mind that God may well not want us knowing every detail of the future until it occurs—but occur it will. Above all, Revelation is a book of worship, describing God's glory and power, authority and plan for all eternity. It makes you sit back and think how small you are, and how great He truly is. By the way, the book of Revelation includes an extremely strong statement against any individual who would ever take away from the Bible's content or choose to add to it. (See Revelation 22:18-19.) There is, therefore, no other book to add to the Bible—no other source we should look toward for spiritual counsel from God. (In addition, the Old Testament contains a severe warning to this same end in Deuteronomy 4:2.) In reading God's Word, here's the point: It's the Bible, only the Bible, all of the Bible, and nothing but the Bible.

# In Closing

*"But be doers of the Word,
and not hearers only, deceiving yourselves."*
**James 1:22**

What else can I say? I think that finally wraps things up. Thanks for joining me for this journey into God's Word! You, too, can be "Wowed!" by all God has to say and how His Word can amazingly impact your life. You have endured my humor, anecdotes, and coffee-filled comments. Congratulations on making it through and living to tell about it. Now don't just sit there; pick up your Bible! There's nothing in this world even remotely like it!

—Mark Cedar
Palm Desert, California

# Appendix

## Chapter Discussion Questions

*"Your Word is a lamp to my feet
and a light to my path."*
**Psalm 119:105**

On the remaining pages, questions are provided which relate to each chapter. These questions are intended for encouraging lively group discussion or toward personal reflection.

**Questions / Chapter 1**

1. When were you first exposed to the Bible's content? (Describe details.)

2. What's your view of the Bible claiming to be the Word of God? (Be honest.)

3. What most fascinates you about the content of the Bible (history, words of wisdom, reported miracles, prophecies, etc.)?

4. What top criticisms of the Bible have you heard? How would you respond?

5. Do you trust a current Bible in its content? Why or why not?

## Questions / Chapter 2

1. Have you ever heard a criticism of the Bible's reliability? Describe it.

2. Would you more readily believe a book's content-claims based upon its singularity of authorship, or would you have more confidence in a text substantiated through many writers?

3. The Bible claims an inspired, divine authorship. How does its authorship and compilation of books differ from other religious texts and their claims to divine authority?

4. What most convinces you to trust the content of the Bible? Conversely, what may be holding you back from trusting it?

5. How would you argue the Bible's claim of being God's Word?

## Questions / Chapter 3

1. What relationship(s) in your life most developed your ability to trust?

2. When the Bible claims to be God's true and perfect Word, how do respond? Is trusting the Bible's content difficult for you?

3. Have you had your trust or confidence broken? How did it impact you?

4. Can you recall a time the Bible spoke directly to you in your life?

5. How can you chart your personal development in trusting the Word of God?

**Questions / Chapter 4**

1. Can you describe an activity which you once enjoyed, but is now routine?

2. When you relate with others, how does their enthusiasm and engagement in conversation improve your time together?

3. Have you ever considered the Bible as being a "living" book? How can this affect the way you read it?

4. Can you describe a topic from the Bible which recently jumped out at you and drew you in?

5. When you read the Bible, can you relate personally? Why or why not?

## Questions / Chapter 5

1. How would you summarize the central message of the Bible?

2. Why does God describe our disobedience against Him in His book?

3. Can you think of a verse which describes God's love for us?

4. Read John, chapter 3 and verse 16. What is God saying to us in this verse?

5. Have you come to believe that Jesus is God's Son, and that He came to save you from your sins?

## Questions / Chapter 6

1. When you're not well, what food tastes best (or helps you most)?

2. Do you have a strict diet, or have you removed certain foods from your personal menu? Why or why not?

3. How can getting the Word of God into your life make a healthy difference?

4. What strategy can you employ to get more of the Bible into you?

5. Do you have a regular time set aside for Bible reading? Have you ever developed the habit of memorizing Scripture?

*Appendix*

**Questions / Chapter 7**

1. Can you think of a first crush or someone you cared for deeply growing up?

2. How has love impacted your life (people, activities, profession)?

3. What have you learned about love through your life experience?

4. Do you believe God loves you? How much do you believe He cares for you?

5. What are the advantages of loving the Word of God, and how can you develop a greater love for it?

**Questions / Chapter 8**

1. Did you receive an allowance growing up, or perhaps receive a special gift in your youth? How did being the recipient of benefits feel?

2. How aware are you of the benefits God offers?

3. Does considering God's benefits help motivate you to read the Bible?

4. When you read the Bible, are you looking for the good in its pages?

5. What promise (benefit) from God means a great deal to you right now?

## Questions / Chapter 9

1. Have you been forced to face some hard news? How did it impact you?

2. How do you tend to respond when confronted by the tough stuff of life?

3. Do you have a "cause" that you stand for? What convictions hold true for you?

4. What standards which God shares in His Word are difficult to accept? Why?

5. Can you think of a time when God confronted you about an action or attitude in your life that needed to change? How did you feel? What did you do?

## Questions / Chapter 10

1. Can you list in order your five top daily habits?

2. What new habit would you like to see added to your daily life?

3. Do you have a time daily in God's Word? If so, describe it.

4. What advantages can you see coming with a daily Bible time?

5. Are you ready to keep a daily Bible time with God? Why or why not?

*Appendix*

## Questions / Chapter 11

1. What is the first Bible verse you can ever remember hearing?

2. Do you have a favorite Bible verse that you can quote?

3. If you needed help from the Bible in a particular way, do you know where you'd look?

4. Can you think of a verse that spoke into your life during a time of discouragement, difficulty or danger?

5. How do you reference special verses of Scripture that speak into your life? (Highlight or underline in your Bible, jot down Scripture reference, make a note in a journal, etc.)

## Questions / Chapter 12

1. When someone suggests reading the Bible, does its size concern you?

2. If you were to commit to reading any one book of the Bible, which would it be? Why?

3. Have you ever read through the complete story of Jesus' life on earth, either in Matthew, Mark, Luke or John?

4. Do you prefer the comfort and encouragement of the book of Psalms, or the wisdom and insight of the book of Proverbs? Why?

5. Have you ever thought about reading through the Bible in a year? Perhaps you would consider going through the New Testament in a year?

www.ingramcontent.com/pod-product-compliance
Lightning Source LLC
Chambersburg PA
CBHW070208100426
42743CB00013B/3101